AF687636

Computer Application For Business: A Practical 360° Approach

NotesKaro

Published by NotesKaro Inc, 2025.

COMPUTER APPLICATION FOR BUSINESS: A PRACTICAL 360° APPROACH

First edition. May 24, 2025.

ISBN: 979-8231687572

Written by NotesKaro.

Table of Contents

Chapter 1: Digital Freelancing for Business Students

In today's digital economy, freelancing has emerged as one of the most powerful ways for students to earn money, build professional skills, and gain real-world experience while still in college. This chapter is specifically designed for business students who want to learn the art of freelancing in a structured, practical, and easy-to-apply way. We will explore freelancing platforms, how to create a successful profile, build gigs, handle payments, communicate with clients, and most importantly, use your business knowledge to provide real value in the market.

What is Digital Freelancing?

DIGITAL FREELANCING refers to offering professional services to clients online, without being tied to a long-term contract or a physical office. You can work from anywhere, on your own schedule, and choose the kind of work you love to do. Freelancing is not just for writers and designers—business students can excel in this space too, offering skills like data entry, Excel modeling, research writing, social media management, and even business planning.

Why Should Business Students Freelance?

- **Real-World Experience:** Freelancing gives you a chance to work on actual client projects and understand market demands.

- **Flexible Earning:** Earn money without disturbing your college schedule.
- **Skill Enhancement:** Apply classroom knowledge to solve real business problems.
- **Portfolio Building:** Create a strong digital resume and work portfolio that helps with future job placements or entrepreneurship.

Top Platforms for Freelancers

1. Fiverr

- FIVERR ALLOWS FREELANCERS to create "gigs"—service offerings with a fixed price.
- Best for beginners. You set your own packages, and buyers come to you.

2. Upwork

- UPWORK IS A MORE formal platform where freelancers bid on jobs posted by clients.
- Ideal for intermediate to advanced freelancers looking for long-term clients.

3. Freelancer.com

- SIMILAR TO UPWORK, but with more competitions and contests.

- Good platform to explore if you're confident in competing with experienced freelancers.

Setting Up Your Profile (First Impressions Matter)

- **Profile Picture:** Use a clean, professional-looking photo.

- **Title:** Be specific: "Excel Data Analyst | Business Researcher | Financial Modeler."

- **Description:** Describe what you offer in a friendly and confident tone.

- **Skills:** List skills that match your field, e.g., Microsoft Excel, Financial Analysis, Business Strategy, Market Research.

Example Profile Snippet: "I'm a business student with a strong foundation in financial analysis, Excel modeling, and market research. I've helped startups and small businesses streamline their data and grow their operations through simple, smart business solutions."

Creating Gigs That Sell

ON FIVERR, GIGS ARE your products. A good gig includes:

- A catchy title: "I will create powerful Excel dashboards for your business."

- Detailed description: What's included? How long will it take?
- Packages: Basic, Standard, Premium
- FAQs: Answer common doubts upfront
- Gallery: Add work samples or a demo video

Example Gigs for Business Students:

- "I will organize your business data in Excel"
- "I will write a market research report on your industry"
- "I will create a PowerPoint pitch deck for your startup"

Managing Payments & Pricing

- START SMALL: OFFER competitive prices when you begin.
- Understand platform fees: Fiverr takes 20%; Upwork charges based on earnings.
- Withdraw safely: Use PayPal or direct bank transfer options.

Tip: As your reviews grow, raise your prices confidently.

Client Communication: Professionalism Wins

FREELANCING SUCCESS depends heavily on how well you communicate.

- Be polite and quick in responses
- Ask clear questions to understand the task fully

• Use simple, error-free English

Message Example: "Hi [Client Name], thank you for considering my services! I've gone through your requirements and I'm confident I can deliver this project within 3 days. I'd love to know more about [specific point]. Looking forward to your reply!"

Real Use-Case Examples for Business Students

1. EXCEL PROJECT FOR a Bakery Business: A student helped a bakery automate their inventory and sales records using Excel formulas and charts. The client paid $60 for a dashboard that took 5 hours to create.

2. Market Research for an Online Clothing Store: Using Google Trends and basic competitor analysis, a freelancer prepared a research document for a fashion startup. Earned $75 and later got hired for monthly reports.

3. Resume Writing & LinkedIn Optimization: Another student offered a gig for "business resume writing." In 2 weeks, he helped 10 clients and made $250 total.

Tips for Growing Fast

• **Niche Down:** Instead of offering "Excel Services," offer "Excel for Business Reports."

• **Overdeliver:** Give something extra—like a bonus tip or design touch.

• **Ask for Reviews:** Politely ask satisfied clients to leave a review.

- **Stay Active:** Log in daily, update gigs, and keep learning.

Common Mistakes to Avoid

- TAKING ALL PROJECTS even if you're unsure—only accept what you can deliver well
- Being slow in replies or ignoring revisions
- Copy-pasting from the internet—plagiarism can ruin your reputation

Chapter 2: Building a Personal Brand on LinkedIn

In the ever-evolving landscape of professional success, personal branding has become the currency of opportunity—and LinkedIn stands at the forefront of that revolution. For business students aspiring to leave a mark, this platform is more than just a digital resume; it's your gateway to networks, internships, freelance gigs, and lifelong professional relationships.

Let's dive deep into the essentials of building an impactful personal brand on LinkedIn, supported by real-world strategies, creative examples, and practical implementation techniques.

1. Understanding Personal Branding on LinkedIn

YOUR PERSONAL BRAND is how the world perceives you professionally. It's not just your name or designation, but the complete story you tell about who you are, what you do, and what value you bring to the table.

On LinkedIn, this story unfolds across your profile, your posts, your engagements, and even the way you message someone. Every action is a brushstroke on the canvas of your professional identity.

2. LinkedIn Profile Optimization

A STRONG PROFILE IS the foundation of your brand. Here's how to structure it for maximum visibility and engagement:

a. Professional Profile Picture:

- Use a clear, high-quality headshot.

- Dress in a way that reflects your industry (business casual works well for students).

b. Headline that Sells: Avoid generic terms like "Student at XYZ College." Instead, write something value-driven:

"Aspiring Business Analyst | Excel Enthusiast | Learning Digital Marketing & Data Visualization"

c. About Section: This is your elevator pitch in written form. Highlight your passion, skills, achievements, and career goals. Keep it crisp, yet authentic.

Example:

"I'm a business student passionate about turning raw data into real insights. From building dashboards in Excel to helping small brands optimize their digital presence, I thrive on learning and applying modern business tools. Currently open to internships and collaborations in digital marketing, business analytics, and freelancing projects."

d. Experience & Projects: Don't worry if you don't have formal work experience. Include freelance gigs, student-led projects, internships, volunteer work, or even personal projects.

e. Skills & Endorsements: Add relevant skills like Excel, PowerPoint, Google Analytics, Digital Marketing, Content Creation, etc. Ask peers to endorse your strongest skills.

f. Certifications: Add any free or paid certifications you've completed from platforms like Coursera, Google, HubSpot, or LinkedIn Learning.

g. Custom URL: Edit your LinkedIn URL to be clean and memorable: linkedin.com/in/yourname

---

3. Business Networking & Content Creation

LINKEDIN IS NOT JUST for reading articles; it's for being seen and heard. Here's how to engage smartly:

a. Connect with Purpose:

- Don't blindly send requests. Add a note like:

"Hi [Name], I'm a business student learning about digital marketing and analytics. Loved your recent post on Excel shortcuts! Would love to connect and learn from your journey."

b. Engage with Content:

- Like, comment on, and share posts that align with your interests.

- Provide thoughtful comments—add value.

c. Create Your Own Content: Not sure what to post? Try:

- Key takeaways from a webinar or certification
- Short tutorials or tips (e.g., Excel shortcuts)
- Lessons from a college project or freelance experience
- A short opinion post about a trending business topic

Example Post:

Just wrapped up a Google Ads certification! Learned how even small ad tweaks can boost ROI significantly. Can't wait to apply this in real campaigns. #DigitalMarketing #LearningJourney

d. Use Hashtags & Emojis Sparingly: Add 3-5 hashtags relevant to your post. Use emojis only to highlight key points, not to decorate.

---

4. Leveraging LinkedIn for Opportunities

ONCE YOUR PROFILE IS polished and you're active, LinkedIn becomes a magnet for opportunities.

a. Finding Internships & Freelance Work:

- Use the "Jobs" tab and apply filters like 'Remote' and 'Internship'.
- Search for posts with hashtags like #InternshipAlert, #FreelanceOpportunity

b. Showcasing Your Work:

- Add your portfolio link (if any) in the Featured section.

- Share screenshots or results of projects you've worked on.

c. Collaborations & Referrals:

- Build real relationships. Don't ask for referrals upfront.

- Support others, and they'll support you.

Example: One student created weekly posts about Excel tips. A startup founder noticed and offered a paid internship to handle spreadsheet modeling for their business.

---

5. Tips to Stand Out as a Student

- **Be consistent:** Post once a week and comment daily.

- **Be specific:** Instead of "Looking for work," write "Open to freelance content writing and Excel-based projects."

- **Be helpful:** Tag peers in opportunities, recommend useful content, and build community.

- **Be authentic:** Share your learnings, struggles, and growth. People connect with real stories.

Chapter 3: Automation Tools for Productivity

Introduction

In today's fast-paced business environment, time is more valuable than ever. Whether you're a student managing assignments and part-time work or an entrepreneur juggling multiple projects, automating repetitive tasks can free up precious time and significantly enhance productivity. This chapter introduces you to powerful automation tools like **Zapier**, **IFTTT**, and **Make.com**, teaching you how to set up smart workflows that handle routine tasks efficiently and reliably. Through real-world examples, you'll learn how to integrate these tools into your daily business processes for maximum impact.

What Is Automation in a Business Context?

AUTOMATION REFERS TO using software or tools to complete tasks without human intervention. This includes activities like sending out emails, updating spreadsheets, generating reports, and posting on social media. The goal is to reduce manual work, avoid errors, and save time.

Automation is often achieved by integrating multiple applications using a trigger-and-action model. For example:

- Trigger: A new form submission on Google Forms
- Action: Add a new row in Google Sheets and send a confirmation email to the user

Now, let's dive into three popular automation tools.

1. Zapier

ZAPIER is an automation tool that connects over 3,000 apps, allowing them to work together without any coding knowledge. It uses simple workflows called "Zaps."

Key Features:

- Connect apps like Gmail, Slack, Google Sheets, Trello, Mailchimp
- Trigger-based automation (e.g., when a new email is received, create a task)
- Multi-step workflows

Example Workflow: Let's say you run a small business and receive customer inquiries through a Google Form. Here's a simple Zap you can create:

- **Trigger**: New response in Google Forms
- **Action 1**: Add customer details to a Google Sheet
- **Action 2**: Send a personalized email to the customer via Gmail

Why it's useful: This saves the manual effort of copying responses, maintaining records, and replying individually.

2. IFTTT (If This Then That)

IFTTT is another easy-to-use automation platform, designed for both personal and business productivity. It connects apps and devices with a simple condition logic: "If this happens, then do that."

Key Features:

- Supports social media, cloud storage, calendars, IoT devices
- Location-based actions (e.g., when I enter office Wi-Fi, mute my phone)
- Voice command integration via Alexa or Google Assistant

Example Workflow: You want to maintain a log of every tweet your company posts:

- **Trigger**: New tweet by your business account
- **Action**: Append the tweet to a Google Sheet

Why it's useful: Helps maintain content records for reporting or analytics without manual effort.

3. Make.com (Formerly Integromat)

MAKE.COM is a more advanced platform that allows detailed workflow automation. It is perfect for users who want to design visual workflows.

Key Features:

- Visual flow editor
- Complex branching, scheduling, and error handling
- Supports thousands of apps and APIs

Example Workflow: You manage an e-commerce store and want to automate order tracking:

- **Trigger**: New order in Shopify
- **Action 1**: Update inventory in Google Sheets
- **Action 2**: Send an order confirmation email via Gmail
- **Action 3**: Notify the packing team via Slack

Why it's useful: Keeps multiple departments in sync without constant communication.

Real-Life Use Cases for Students and Entrepreneurs

1. **Email Management**: Automatically categorize incoming client emails, label them, and send canned responses.
2. **Content Publishing**: Auto-post your new blog or

YouTube content to Facebook, LinkedIn, or Twitter.

3. **Data Entry**: Collect survey results in Google Forms and auto-populate your CRM or spreadsheet.
4. **Reminders**: Automatically send daily task reminders to your team using Slack or WhatsApp integrations.

Tips for Creating Effective Workflows

• **Start Simple**: Begin with a one-step workflow and test its reliability.

• **Use Templates**: Zapier and IFTTT offer pre-built automation templates.

• **Monitor Logs**: Check the history of your automations to troubleshoot errors.

• **Avoid Redundancy**: Don't create overlapping workflows; keep it lean.

Potential Pitfalls and How to Avoid Them

• **Too Many Automations**: Automating everything might make you lose control. Stick to high-frequency tasks.

• **Broken Triggers**: Always test workflows before relying on them. App updates may change APIs or integration support.

• **Data Privacy**: Be mindful of what kind of data you're automating. Never expose sensitive business/client information.

Summary

MASTERING AUTOMATION tools like Zapier, IFTTT, and Make.com is like having a virtual assistant who never sleeps. They simplify your life, reduce errors, and give you more time to focus on growth, creativity, and decision-making. In the next chapter, we'll dive into another powerful layer of business enhancement — **Digital Accounting Tools** — where automation also plays a major role.

Chapter 4: No-Code Tools to Build Business Apps & Websites

In today's fast-paced digital economy, not every business owner or student has time to learn traditional programming. The rise of **no-code tools** has transformed how we build digital products, enabling individuals to create powerful apps and websites without writing a single line of code. These tools are perfect for startups, freelancers, and students who want to build fast, test ideas, and solve real business problems.

What Are No-Code Tools?

NO-CODE TOOLS ARE PLATFORMS that allow users to build software applications or websites using graphical user interfaces instead of programming languages. They simplify development and open the door to digital creation for non-technical users.

Why Are No-Code Tools Important for Business Students?

- **Cost-effective**: No need to hire developers.
- **Speed**: Launch projects in days, not months.
- **Testing ideas**: Validate business concepts without investing heavily.

- **Skill development**: Learn digital tools relevant for the future workforce.

Let's explore some of the most popular and powerful no-code tools you can use today.

1. Notion: Your All-in-One Workspace

WHAT IT IS: A tool for notes, task management, and database creation.

Use Case:

- Build a **CRM (Customer Relationship Management)** for your startup.
- Create a **content calendar** for marketing.
- Maintain a **personal portfolio or project tracker**.

Example: You can create a table in Notion with columns like Name, Email, Last Contact Date, and Notes to track your business leads.

Why it's great:

- Beautiful UI
- Real-time collaboration
- Easily embeddable in websites

2. Glide: Create Mobile Apps from Google Sheets

WHAT IT IS: Glide converts a Google Sheet into a mobile-friendly app.

Use Case:

- Inventory tracker for a small business
- Student attendance app
- Event registration form and check-in tool

Example: Maintain your stock in a Google Sheet. Glide will turn that data into a fully functional inventory management app.

Why it's great:

- No learning curve
- Great for internal use
- Share your app via link or QR code

---

3. Softr: Build Business Apps & Portals Using Airtable

WHAT IT IS: A no-code platform that turns your Airtable databases into full-fledged web apps.

Use Case:

- Job board for your college
- Membership portal for your startup

- Team task dashboard

Example: If you're collecting job listings in Airtable, Softr can turn it into a browsable job board website in a few minutes.

Why it's great:

- Tight integration with Airtable
- Ready-made templates
- User authentication built-in

4. Carrd: Build Beautiful One-Page Websites

WHAT IT IS: Carrd is a simple platform to create one-page websites quickly.

Use Case:

- Personal resume site
- Startup landing page
- Event registration page

Example: In under 30 minutes, you can have a personal website showcasing your bio, achievements, and contact form.

Why it's great:

- Extremely easy to use
- Very affordable (free & pro versions)
- Mobile responsive

5. Canva Sites: Design-Led Website Builder

WHAT IT IS: Known for graphic design, Canva now lets users build basic websites too.

Use Case:

- Event microsites
- Student project showcase
- Business service landing page

Example: You can create a website for your final-year college event with Canva and embed photos, RSVP forms, and team details.

Why it's great:

- Drag-and-drop simplicity
- No need for technical knowledge
- Stylish templates

Real Business Use-Cases

LET'S SEE HOW THESE tools are being used by students and startups:

1. **Mini CRM in Notion**: A student freelancer tracks all his design clients in a Notion table, sorted by deadlines.
2. **Inventory Tracker in Glide**: A local bakery tracks its

daily ingredients and stock using a Glide app.

3. **Portfolio Website on Carrd**: A college student builds a one-pager to showcase his resume, certifications, and projects to recruiters.
4. **Internship Job Board with Softr**: A campus club lists and manages internships using Airtable + Softr.
5. **Canva Site for a Project**: A group makes a project website in Canva with infographics and video presentations.

Conclusion

NO-CODE TOOLS ARE THE bridge between your ideas and execution. They empower students and entrepreneurs to become creators, not just consumers. Whether it's launching your brand, managing clients, or building tools for your business, these platforms offer everything you need — with zero coding knowledge required.

Tip: Don't just read about these tools — try building something simple today. The best way to learn is by doing.

Chapter 5: AI Tools in Business

In today's rapidly transforming digital world, Artificial Intelligence (AI) is no longer a distant concept—it is an active, everyday part of how modern businesses operate. From writing emails to designing visuals, AI tools have become vital companions for business professionals seeking efficiency, creativity, and strategic edge. In this chapter, we'll explore how AI tools such as ChatGPT, Copy.ai, Midjourney, Grammarly, and others are transforming the business ecosystem—and how you, as a student or entrepreneur, can responsibly and effectively integrate them into your workflow.

Understanding AI in Business

AI REFERS TO THE SIMULATION of human intelligence by machines. These systems learn from data, identify patterns, and make decisions with minimal human intervention. While traditional automation simply follows commands, AI evolves and improves over time, making it ideal for dynamic business needs.

Key AI Tools and Their Uses

1. ChatGPT (OpenAI)

- **Use:** Writing emails, customer responses, business content, social media captions, brainstorming ideas, summarizing research.

- **Example:** Imagine you're preparing a pitch deck for your startup. You can use ChatGPT to generate compelling taglines, structure your content, and even prepare sample Q&A for your investor meeting.

2. Copy.ai

- **Use:** AI-based marketing copywriting tool that generates ad content, blogs, slogans, and email templates.

- **Example:** A student launching a product on Instagram can use Copy.ai to write product descriptions, welcome messages, or even generate a product story in seconds.

3. Midjourney

- **Use:** AI image generation—great for presentations, posters, branding, and social media campaigns.

- **Example:** Instead of hiring a graphic designer for every poster, students can use Midjourney to generate promotional banners with custom prompts and tweak designs on the go.

4. Grammarly

● **Use:** Real-time grammar correction, tone detection, and writing improvement.

● **Example:** Writing a business proposal? Grammarly helps ensure professional tone, clarity, and precision—vital for winning clients or impressing professors.

5. Other Emerging AI Tools

● **Pictory:** Converts text into video—perfect for marketing or educational content.

● **Runway ML:** Video editing with AI enhancements.

● **Tome:** AI-powered presentation creator—ideal for business meetings and academic projects.

AI in Real Business Scenarios

1. **Writing & Research:** AI can help draft business emails, generate insights from market research, or create social media calendars.
2. **Presentations & Reports:** AI tools like Tome or Canva AI allow you to create stunning decks and visualize data without spending hours on design.
3. **Planning & Strategy:** ChatGPT and similar models help you brainstorm business models, analyze customer feedback, or generate marketing plans.

Responsible Use of AI

WHILE AI CAN BE AN incredible assistant, using it ethically is critical:

• **Don't plagiarize:** Always revise and humanize AI-generated content.

• **Respect privacy:** Never feed confidential business data into AI models.

• **Cross-check facts:** AI sometimes hallucinates—always verify facts.

• **Give credit when due:** Transparency builds trust, especially in team environments.

Practical Business Workflow with AI

LET'S SAY YOU RUN A small digital marketing service:

1. **Client Onboarding Email** – Drafted using ChatGPT.
2. **Client Proposal Document** – Polished with Grammarly.
3. **Instagram Visual Posts** – Created with Midjourney.
4. **Email Campaign Copy** – Generated through Copy.ai.
5. **Progress Report Presentation** – Built with Tome.

You just saved 70% of your time while maintaining professionalism and creativity.

Chapter 6: Digital Payments & UPI Ecosystem

In today's digital-first economy, managing money online is no longer a luxury but a necessity. Whether you're a small business owner, a freelancer, or a student entrepreneur, understanding the digital payment ecosystem can help you get paid faster, streamline transactions, and offer more convenience to your customers. This chapter delves into the heart of digital payments in India with a strong focus on the Unified Payments Interface (UPI) and supporting platforms like Google Pay, PhonePe, Paytm, and tools like Razorpay and Cashfree.

---

1. Introduction to Digital Payments

DIGITAL PAYMENTS REFER to the transfer of money through digital or electronic modes, without using physical cash. In India, this revolution was significantly powered by the launch of UPI by the National Payments Corporation of India (NPCI) in 2016.

Why are digital payments important?

- Instant transactions
- Better tracking of income and expenses
- Paperless and cashless convenience

- Secure and scalable for businesses

---

2. Understanding UPI: The Game-Changer

UPI, OR UNIFIED PAYMENTS Interface, enables users to link multiple bank accounts to a single mobile application. It allows money transfers, bill payments, and online purchases directly from your bank account.

Key features of UPI:

- Real-time money transfer
- 24/7 availability
- No need for bank account details (only UPI ID needed)
- Low transaction costs

Example: You're a student selling digital notes. You can share your UPI ID (like yourname@upi) with buyers, and they can instantly pay you.

---

3. Platforms Built on UPI: Google Pay, PhonePe, Paytm

THESE APPS OFFER UPI services with user-friendly interfaces:

- **Google Pay:** Clean design, rewards system, and strong integration with bank accounts.
- **PhonePe:** Great for utility payments, mutual funds, and gold purchases.

- **Paytm:** More than just UPI—wallet, bank, ticket bookings, and bill payments.

Scenario: A college entrepreneur can collect payments using QR codes generated from these apps for things like selling merchandise or organizing events.

---

4. The QR Code Business Model

QR CODES MAKE DIGITAL payments even easier. Businesses can generate a static or dynamic QR code linked to their UPI or bank account.

How it works:

- Static QR: Fixed account, user enters amount
- Dynamic QR: Amount is pre-filled, ideal for billing

Example: A tea stall vendor uses a PhonePe QR code. Customers scan it and pay directly—no need for cash exchange.

Bonus Tip: Small businesses can brand their QR codes with logos using Paytm for Business or Razorpay.

---

5. Bank Linking & Settlement Rules

TO USE UPI, YOUR MOBILE number must be linked to your bank account. Once linked through any UPI app, transactions are processed by NPCI and settled in real-time or within 24 hours, depending on the bank.

Important rules:

- Daily transaction limits (usually Rs. 1 lakh)
- Bank downtime can delay payments
- Keep UPI PIN confidential

---

6. Creating Your Own Payment Gateway (Razorpay/ Cashfree)

FOR MORE PROFESSIONAL or startup-level needs, businesses can set up their own payment gateway using services like **Razorpay** or **Cashfree**.

Steps to create a payment gateway:

1. Sign up on Razorpay or Cashfree
2. Complete KYC verification
3. Generate payment links or embed a gateway on your website
4. Start accepting cards, UPI, wallets, and net banking payments

Example Use-Case: If you're building a digital course platform, integrate Razorpay on your website to accept one-time and recurring payments.

---

7. Security Best Practices

- ENABLE APP LOCK and UPI PIN security

- Use verified apps (avoid unofficial clones)
- Always check recipient name before paying
- Don't share UPI OTPs or PINs

---

8. Business Advantages of Digital Payments

- BETTER CASH FLOW tracking
- No need for a cash register or physical invoices
- Ability to serve customers remotely
- Enhanced trust and brand perception

---

9. Challenges in the Ecosystem

- INTERNET DEPENDENCY
- Fraud and phishing attempts
- App crashes or technical downtime

Solution: Combine UPI with a traditional POS (Point of Sale) or accept multiple forms of payment.

---

10. The Future of Digital Payments

WITH RBI PROMOTING digital banking and innovations like e-RUPI, CBDC (Central Bank Digital Currency), and offline UPI, the future is cashless, fast, and efficient.

Chapter 7: Project Management Tools for Teams

In today's fast-paced and highly collaborative business environments, effective project management has become an essential skill—not only in corporations but also for students, freelancers, and startup founders. Managing tasks, responsibilities, deadlines, and collaboration can be overwhelming without the right tools. Fortunately, a wide range of intuitive and powerful project management platforms is now available that don't require any technical expertise.

This chapter will explore some of the most effective and accessible project management tools—**Trello**, **Asana**, **Notion**, and **ClickUp**—along with practical ways to use them for student projects, startup planning, and team coordination. Whether you're planning a college fest, launching a new startup product, or collaborating on a research paper, these tools will help streamline your workflow and improve team accountability.

1. Why Project Management Tools Matter

BEFORE JUMPING INTO tools, let's understand what project management tools solve:

- Keeping everyone aligned and aware of their tasks
- Meeting deadlines through proper scheduling

- Tracking task progress to avoid delays
- Documenting communication and responsibilities
- Avoiding chaos in multitasking environments

Without such tools, projects are vulnerable to confusion, missed deadlines, and poor outcomes.

---

2. Trello – Visual Kanban Boards for Simplicity

USE-CASE: Group assignment coordination

Trello works on a visual "board and card" system. Think of a whiteboard with sticky notes—that's what Trello replicates digitally.

Key Features:

- BOARDS, LISTS, AND Cards structure
- Drag-and-drop task movement
- Checklists, attachments, comments
- Due dates, color labels, and members tagging

Example:

LET'S SAY YOU'RE LEADING a team working on a research report. You create a Trello board with columns like **To Do**, **Doing**, and **Done**. Each task like "Research Topic," "Collect

Data," "Draft Writing" becomes a card. Assign teammates, set deadlines, and watch progress move visually.

Trello Pro Tip:

USE TRELLO POWER-UPS like **Calendar view** or **Butler automation** for scheduling and automation.

3. Asana – Timeline-Driven Professional Projects

USE-CASE: Startup project planning

Asana is more detailed and structured. It's ideal when you have dependencies (task A must finish before task B starts).

Key Features:

- TIMELINE (GANTT-style) views
- Task dependencies and subtasks
- Milestones and goals
- Workload view for resource planning

Example:

YOU'RE LAUNCHING A digital product in 30 days. With Asana, map every task—from designing to marketing—and assign deadlines. You can mark which tasks depend on others, so delays automatically reflect across the timeline.

Asana Pro Tip:

USE THE **Form feature** to allow team members to submit task requests that automatically land in your board.

---

4. Notion – All-in-One Workspace

USE-CASE: Student startup dashboard

Notion combines notes, databases, calendars, and to-do lists in one place. Its flexibility makes it ideal for those who want everything—ideas, links, tasks, files—in one page.

Key Features:

- PAGES, TEMPLATES, and linked databases
- Task boards, calendars, and wikis
- Embed Google Drive, Figma, YouTube, etc.

Example:

YOU RUN A STUDENT-LED clothing brand. Use Notion to create a page for your product catalog, another for supplier contacts, and one for marketing tasks. You can link databases to see progress and collaborate seamlessly.

Notion Pro Tip:

USE **pre-built templates** like “Startup OS” or “Weekly Planner” to save setup time.

---

5. ClickUp – Everything Under One Roof

USE-CASE: Freelance project collaboration

ClickUp is the powerhouse—suited for professionals who want everything from document writing to bug tracking in a single app.

Key Features:

- LISTS, BOARDS, CALENDAR, Gantt, and box views
- Time tracking and workload management
- Integrated docs, goals, chat
- Customizable statuses

Example:

YOU'RE A FREELANCE team building a website. ClickUp lets you write the content directly in its Docs feature, create sprints, track bugs, and discuss inside tasks—no need for separate tools.

ClickUp Pro Tip:

USE **automation rules** (like moving tasks when completed) and **goal tracking** to stay focused on outcomes.

6. How Students Can Use These Tools Practically

- **College Events:** Use Trello or Notion to assign roles for volunteers, create checklists for logistics, and track sponsorships.
- **Assignments:** Use Asana to divide sections of a group project and schedule reviews.
- **Startup Teams:** Use ClickUp to track product development, content marketing, and customer feedback in one place.
- **Internship Work:** Show professionalism by maintaining a Notion dashboard to report weekly updates and goals.

7. Choosing the Right Tool

Tool	Best For	Learning Curve	Free Plan
Trello	Beginners & visual users	Low	Yes
Asana	Structured projects	Medium	Yes
Notion	Creative documentation	Medium	Yes
ClickUp	Power users & teams	High	Yes

8. Final Thoughts

MASTERING PROJECT MANAGEMENT tools early gives you a career advantage. These platforms make teamwork smooth, timelines manageable, and outcomes more predictable. Even if your projects are small now, using these tools builds habits that prepare you for high-pressure corporate or startup environments.

Don't wait for a professor or boss to teach you. Start using these tools today for your personal goals, assignments, and freelance work. You'll be surprised how organized, confident, and efficient your digital workspace becomes.

Pro Tip: Try combining tools! For example, use Notion for documentation + Trello for tasks + Google Calendar for deadlines.

"A good tool doesn't just manage work—it inspires great work."

Chapter 8: Understanding GST, Invoicing & Business Compliance

In today's digital and entrepreneurial era, understanding the fundamentals of taxation and invoicing is crucial for every aspiring business owner, freelancer, and service provider. This chapter simplifies the complex world of Goods and Services Tax (GST), digital invoicing, and compliance through real-world tools and examples to help you confidently manage the financial and legal side of your business.

---

1. What is GST?

GST STANDS FOR GOODS and Services Tax, a unified indirect tax levied on the supply of goods and services in India. It replaced multiple taxes like VAT, excise duty, and service tax, making tax compliance easier.

Key Features of GST:

- **One Nation, One Tax**: Uniform tax structure across India

- **Destination-Based**: Tax collected where goods/services are consumed

- **Multiple Slabs**: 0%, 5%, 12%, 18%, and 28%

- **CGST, SGST, IGST**: Based on intra-state or inter-state supply

2. Who Needs to Register for GST?

YOU NEED GST REGISTRATION if:

- Your **turnover exceeds Rs. 20 lakh** (Rs. 10 lakh in NE states)
- You are selling goods or services **across state borders**
- You are selling through **online marketplaces**
- You are a **freelancer or consultant** providing services above the threshold limit

Even if you don't meet the threshold, **voluntary registration** helps in building credibility and availing input tax credits.

---

3. E-Invoicing and Digital Billing

MODERN BUSINESSES USE software for automated and legally compliant billing. Here are some digital tools you can use:

a. Vyapar App

- DESIGNED FOR SMALL Indian businesses
- Generate GST-compliant invoices in Hindi/English
- Track inventory, sales, and profit

b. Zoho Invoice

- CLEAN UI WITH GST-compliant templates
- Easy recurring invoice generation
- Connects with payment gateways

c. TallyPrime

- TRADITIONAL ACCOUNTING + GST solution
- Preferred by CA firms and retailers

d. Refrens

- GREAT FOR FREELANCERS and agencies
- Generate contracts, invoices, and receive payments

---

4. How to File GST Returns?

GST RETURNS ARE DOCUMENTS that contain your sales, purchases, tax collected, and tax paid.

Basic Returns:

- **GSTR-1**: Details of outward supplies (monthly)
- **GSTR-3B**: Summary return of tax liabilities (monthly)
- **GSTR-4**: For composition scheme users

Steps:

1. Login tohttps://www.gst.gov.in
2. Upload invoices and match with GSTR-2A
3. File returns using OTP verification

TOOLS LIKE **ClearTax** or **Khatabook GST** can simplify this process with pre-filled data and reminders.

5. Common Mistakes to Avoid

• **Missing GST on invoices**: Ensure every invoice includes GST breakdown

• **Wrong GSTIN usage**: Use correct GSTIN for each state

• **Late filing**: Attracts penalty of Rs. 50–100 per day

• **Not claiming ITC** (Input Tax Credit): Reduces your overall tax burden

• **Mixing taxable and exempted goods**: Should be clearly separated

6. When Do You NOT Need GST?

• IF YOU'RE DOING **freelancing under Rs. 20 lakh turnover**

• If you sell only **unregistered services** within your state

• If you are a **student entrepreneur** testing an idea

However, always check latest updates as rules change frequently.

7. Use Case: Freelance Designer with GST

RITIKA, A FREELANCE graphic designer in Delhi, earns about Rs. 5 lakh annually through Fiverr and Upwork. Since her turnover is below Rs. 20 lakh and all her work is online and within India, she doesn't need GST registration now. But once she crosses the threshold or starts working with clients abroad, she'll opt for registration to avoid legal issues and gain trust.

8. Pro Tips for Young Entrepreneurs

- USE **digital invoicing** for professionalism
- Keep records of every transaction (Google Sheets/Notion)
- Learn basic tax terms even if you have an accountant
- Use **UPI/QR Code** with business name for payments
- Get your **PAN & bank account** linked properly with your business name

Chapter 9: Digital File & Document Management

In the fast-paced digital business environment, efficient file and document management is a game-changer. Whether you're working solo, in a startup, or within a large organization, having a clear and effective system to store, manage, and share files can save you from hours of confusion, lost data, or poor collaboration.

1. Why Digital File Management Matters

BUSINESSES RUN ON DATA. Contracts, financial records, customer details, marketing plans—everything is digital. Poor management can lead to lost files, privacy issues, duplication of work, and inefficiency.

2. Cloud Storage Tools Overview

LET'S EXPLORE THE MOST widely used digital storage tools:

- **Google Drive**: Integrated with Gmail and Google Workspace, supports Docs, Sheets, Slides. Great for collaboration.

- **OneDrive**: Best for businesses using Microsoft Office tools. Syncs with Word, Excel, PowerPoint.

• **Dropbox**: Known for its simplicity and sharing capabilities. Often used for media and large file storage.

These platforms offer free storage (up to a limit), easy sharing options, and accessibility from any device.

3. Folder Structure for Business

A WELL-THOUGHT-OUT folder structure ensures that files are easy to locate. Here's a simple example for a small business:

```
BusinessName/
├── Admin/
│ ├── Licenses
│ ├── Registrations
├── Finance/
│ ├── Invoices
│ ├── Receipts
├── Projects/
│ ├── Project A
│ ├── Project B
├── Marketing/
│ ├── Graphics
│ ├── Campaigns
```

Customize this structure based on your needs, but keep it clean and consistent.

4. File Naming Conventions

AVOID FILES NAMED FINALFINALCOPY.docx or invoice123.pdf with no dates. Use naming conventions that are clear and searchable. Example:

- Invoice_ClientName_2025-03-10.pdf
- Proposal_ProjectA_2025-05.docx

Use underscores or hyphens instead of spaces, and always add dates in YYYY-MM-DD format for sorting.

5. Data Backups and Version Control

DON'T JUST RELY ON cloud syncing—make regular backups:

- Weekly or monthly local backups on external hard drives.
- Use version history features on Google Drive and OneDrive to track edits and revert to earlier versions.
- Use apps like Backblaze or Carbonite for automated backups.

6. Sharing & Access Rights

SHARING IS EASY—BUT security matters.

- Use "View Only" links for public access.
- Give "Editor" access only when needed.

- In shared drives, use folder-level permissions so people don't access sensitive data by mistake.
- Audit sharing settings periodically.

7. File Management Automation

USE TOOLS LIKE ZAPIER or Make.com to automate tasks:

- Auto-upload email attachments to specific Drive folders.
- Rename uploaded files using specific triggers.
- Auto-organize weekly report folders.

8. Tips for Long-Term Organization

- SET A MONTHLY CLEANUP day.
- Archive old projects or clients in a separate folder.
- Delete duplicate or unnecessary files.
- Train your team to follow file naming and folder protocols.

9. Real-World Example

IMAGINE A FREELANCE designer who works with 10 clients. They create a folder for each client with subfolders:

```
Clients/
├── Client A/
│ ├── Logos
```

| ├── Feedback

| ├── Final Designs

Every invoice is saved in a Billing folder using the naming format: Invoice_ClientA_2025-04-20.pdf. They share final designs via "View Only" links and archive old clients annually.

Chapter 10: Creating & Selling Digital Products

In today's digital age, creating and selling digital products has become one of the most accessible and profitable ways to start or grow a business. Unlike physical products, digital products require minimal upfront costs, no inventory, and can reach a global audience instantly. This chapter explores how you can create digital products, the platforms to sell them on, and the business models that make digital selling successful.

1. What Are Digital Products?

DIGITAL PRODUCTS ARE intangible goods delivered electronically. Some popular examples include:

- **E-books:** Digital books on topics you are passionate about or expert in.

- **Online Courses:** Video or text-based lessons teaching a skill or knowledge.

- **Templates:** Ready-made designs for resumes, presentations, social media posts, business plans, etc.

- **Designs & Art:** Digital artwork, graphics, icons, logos, or printables.

2. Why Choose Digital Products?

- **Low cost:** No manufacturing or shipping.
- **Scalability:** Sell unlimited copies without restocking.
- **Flexibility:** Work from anywhere.
- **Automation:** Sales and delivery can be automated.

3. Steps to Create Digital Products

A. IDENTIFY YOUR NICHE & Audience:

Choose a niche where you have expertise or interest. Understand your audience's needs by researching forums, social media groups, or surveys.

b. Plan Your Product:

Outline the content for your e-book or course, or design templates that solve a problem or add value.

c. Create the Content:

- For e-books, write clearly with practical advice and engaging examples. Use tools like Microsoft Word, Google Docs, or Canva for formatting.
- For courses, use video recording tools (Zoom, Loom), and platforms like Teachable or Thinkific to host.
- For templates and designs, software like Canva, Adobe Illustrator, or Figma helps craft professional looks.

d. Package & Format:

Ensure your product is user-friendly: PDFs for e-books, MP4 for videos, and ZIP files for templates.

4. Selling Platforms

YOU DON'T HAVE TO BUILD your own website to sell digital products. Some trusted platforms include:

- **Gumroad:** Easy to use, supports subscriptions, and offers marketing tools.
- **Payhip:** Simple store setup with built-in affiliate marketing.
- **Sellfy:** Great for digital and physical products, supports email marketing.

Each platform takes a small commission or monthly fee but handles payment processing, product delivery, and VAT taxes automatically.

5. Business Models for Digital Creators

A. ONE-TIME PURCHASE:

Customers buy the product once and get lifetime access.

b. Subscription:

Offer access to a collection of products or continuous updates for a monthly or yearly fee.

c. Freemium Model:

Provide a free basic version and charge for premium content or features.

d. Bundling:

Combine multiple products (e.g., e-book + templates + course) to increase value and price.

6. Marketing Your Digital Products

- **Social Media:** Share sneak peeks, customer testimonials, and use ads on Facebook, Instagram, or LinkedIn.

- **Email Marketing:** Build an email list to notify customers about new launches and offers.

- **Affiliate Marketing:** Allow others to promote your product for a commission.

- **Content Marketing:** Write blogs, create YouTube videos, or podcasts related to your product's topic.

7. Real-World Example

IMAGINE A MARKETING student creating an e-book titled *"Social Media Marketing for Beginners."* Along with the e-book, they design Instagram post templates and offer a mini-course on creating Facebook ads. They upload everything on Gumroad and promote it via Instagram and LinkedIn. Customers purchase the e-book or the full bundle depending on their needs. As the author updates content and adds new templates, subscribers get notified via email.

8. Challenges and Tips

- **Protecting Your Product:** Use watermarks and restrict file sharing where possible.

- **Customer Support:** Be ready to assist buyers with downloads or usage queries.

- **Continuous Improvement:** Update content based on feedback and trends.

About the Publisher

About NotesKaro Inc.

Introduction

In the digital age, where education is evolving rapidly and students are striving to keep pace with vast syllabi and competitive pressures, a revolutionary academic platform—NotesKaro Inc.—is emerging as a game-changer. Founded by visionary entrepreneur and author Mrigendra Bharti, NotesKaro Inc. operates under the umbrella of Sellbrochure Vymish Entertainment, a pioneering global publishing initiative.

NotesKaro Inc. is designed with a singular aim: to simplify learning by converting complex lecture notes into concise, concept-rich, and uniquely detailed formats that aid faster and deeper understanding. It empowers students from all academic backgrounds to study smart, perform better, and retain knowledge more effectively.

Whether you're preparing for board exams, college semesters, or competitive tests, NotesKaro Inc. brings academic content to your fingertips—easy to grasp, reliable, and tailored to your syllabus.

A Brainchild of Mrigendra Bharti

NotesKaro Inc. is not just another edtech venture. It is a vision-driven initiative by Mrigendra Bharti, a young entrepreneur, author of over 70 books, and founder of India's fastest-growing free publishing house—Sellbrochure Vymish Entertainment.

Mrigendra started NotesKaro out of a personal realization: students across India often struggle to access organized, well-written notes that are both brief and comprehensive. Most materials available are either too lengthy, overly generic, or riddled with outdated content. NotesKaro was born to solve this very problem.

By creating lecture notes that are concise yet carry deep insight, Mrigendra envisioned a platform where quality meets accessibility—and where learning becomes less burdensome and more efficient.

Part of Sellbrochure – A Publishing Giant

As a proud subsidiary of Sellbrochure Vymish Entertainment, NotesKaro Inc. benefits from an international publishing network spread across 220+ global platforms, including digital libraries, educational marketplaces, and bookstores.

This synergy allows NotesKaro to not only create high-quality academic content but also distribute it worldwide in both print and digital formats, ensuring students everywhere can benefit from it. The brand operates under the same core philosophy as Sellbrochure—education without limitations.

What Makes NotesKaro Inc. Unique?

1. Concise but Not Compromised

Unlike other platforms that provide either over-summarized or overly detailed notes, NotesKaro finds the perfect balance. Each set of notes is carefully structured to ensure:

Crisp explanation of core concepts

Easy-to-remember formats

Bullet points, charts, and illustrations

Chapter-wise clarity with sub-topic divisions

This approach helps students revise quickly and retain information longer.

2. Deep Detailing for Conceptual Clarity

Every topic is treated with the importance it deserves. Even within short notes, NotesKaro adds in-depth insights, examples, and real-world connections to ensure students grasp not just what to learn, but also why and how it matters.

Whether it's technical definitions in engineering, case studies in management, or theoretical concepts in humanities—NotesKaro never compromises on the depth of understanding.

Multi-Format Accessibility

NotesKaro's notes are available in:

PDF format for digital reading

Ebooks for Kindle, Kobo, and other platforms

Print on demand via Sellbrochure's global network

Mobile-optimized formats for easy access on the

Why NotesKaro Inc. Matters Today

In a country with over 300 million students, the need for accessible, affordable, and effective academic resources has never been greater. NotesKaro Inc. stands at the intersection of innovation and necessity.

It represents:

Relief from textbook overload

www.ingramcontent.com/pod-product-compliance
Lightning Source LLC
LaVergne TN
LVHW022028200926
848481LV00007B/2592
9798231687572